# Way of *Wakan*

## Reflections on Lakota Spirituality and Grief

By

David J. Mathieu

Way of Wakan:  Reflections on Lakota Spirituality and Grief

Copyright 2013 by David J. Mathieu, Ed.D.

ISBN  978-1481897150

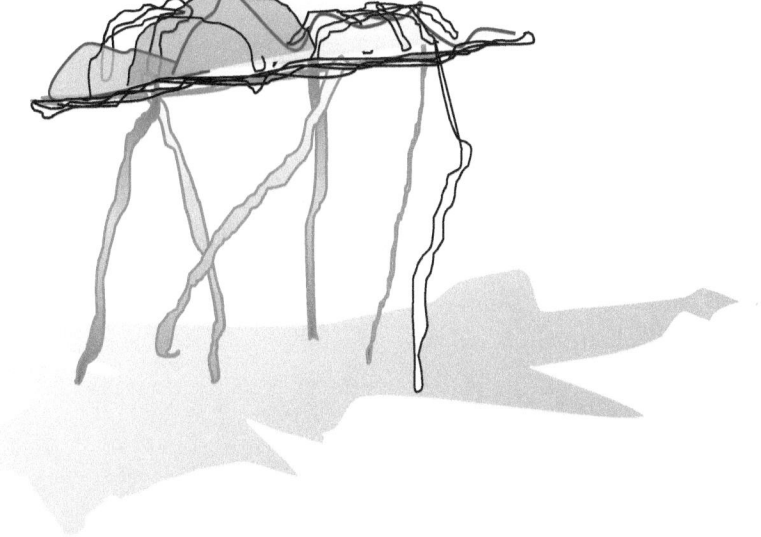

# Dedication

To our beautiful daughter, Felicity Abby Jane Mathieu, who is missed greatly and deeply by our family and her friends. Her spirit is with us and the whole hoop of the world always.

Mitakuye Oyasin
(All My Relatives)

# Acknowledgements

As this narrative is based largely on conversations with them many years ago, I am very thankful to the late Sidney Keith and the late Martin High Bear for sharing with me their knowledge and perspectives on traditional Lakota sacred thought. They were both very special individuals and were highly respected throughout Lakota country.

Many other individuals were critically helpful over the years in helping me arrive at a mature understanding of Lakota language, culture, and other issues and ideas from around Indian country. Some of these important people include Calvin Jumping Bull, Gerald One Feather, Bertha Chasing Hawk, Ronnie Theisz, Monica Garreau, Carrie Schommer, Becky Flute, Maria Decora, Roger Buffalohead, George Morrison, Bob Powless, Ted Mahto, Clara Sue Kidwell, Albert White Hat, Lowell Amiotte, Frank Lawrence, Elgin Badwound, Mary Young, Doris

Leader Charge, Ray Howe, John Gritts, Trudell Guerue, Don Schanandore, and Martin Brokenleg.

Special appreciation goes to my wife and best friend of 40 years, Sue Ann Daley-Mathieu, and my sons Benjamin and Jessua who deeply share the grief over the death of their little sister Felicity. I also very much appreciate Sue Ann's cover and interior design.

Thanks also to a few close friends and colleagues who assisted with the editing of my writing and ideas as well as much encouragement including, in particular, Jeff Zuckerman.

# Contents

# Preface

As a white kid who grew up in Minneapolis, played with Tonka Toy trucks in every available dirt pile, rode his bike fearlessly all over town, made "forts" from discarded lumber every summer, and slept outside in the backyard with friends in all manner of shelters from improvised tents to cardboard boxes, that I would, as an adult, find myself teaching Lakota language and other aspects of American Indian studies in South Dakota and elsewhere still strikes me as pretty startling. This should strike the reader in much the same way.

This book must be seen as information and insight learned second-hand rather than as native. Although I taught Lakota language and other topics in American Indian studies for many years, I have always tried to be humble about my presence in the subject matter as a person who did not come to know this information as a child. Thus, what is presented here is nothing more than what I have learned and applied to the grief of my family following the death of our daughter.

The challenges in the telling of *Way of Wakan* have been significant, but helpful in the telling in many ways as well. The direction of the content has morphed a bit since I began writing, but I am grateful that it has.

I have attempted to provide Lakota translations for the major concepts presented concerning Lakota spirituality. Some of the Lakota terms differ from one part of Lakota country to another.  An example is the word for children, *wakanheja,* which is more often heard on the Cheyenne River reservation and *wakanyeja,* which is heard more often on the Rosebud.

Due to the limitations of letter font in printing and also the burden of consistently providing phonetic spellings, I have used the simple classroom orthography that I used in my Lakota language textbooks.  I have also provided a simple pronunciation guide in the back of the book in order to give the reader some assistance in pronouncing Lakota terms.

As explained in a later section of the book, Lakota verb tenses have different cultural meanings than are used in English. Additionally, the past and the present tenses are not expressly differentiated other than by way of sentence context or time references. My use of tense in the following pages reflects some of this lack of precision that is required in English.

Much of the concepts here were those taught me by medicine men Sidney Keith and Martin High Bear. I also use the word medicine men generically. The reader should note that women often also performed the role particularly with regard to healing and knowledge of traditional medicines. I have chosen, however, to use the male form in deference to traditional usage of the term.

What I have presented reflects the learning I acquired in conversation with the medicine men and through inquiry with other Lakotas. The quotations from Sidney Keith and Martin High Bear are actually reconstructions from memory as well as my rather limited notes.

 I have served no apprenticeship nor have I attempted to be a practitioner of traditional medicine or religion; only as a willing participant when the opportunity arose. There is clearly much more to know than what is presented here.  I have included that information which, I feel, impacts our understanding of death and grief in the non-tribal world as well as being relevant to our journey in understanding the death of our daughter Felicity.

*Way of Wakan* is not intended to be a manual on grief or grief processes. It is my hope, however, that seeing grief from another perspective, another time, and another experience based on a spiritual tradition differing from Christianity will be of help in understanding our common experience with death and grief.

*David J. Mathieu*

*January, 2013*

# Part One: Introduction

## An Unusual Juxtaposition of Experiences: Lakota Spirituality and Felicity Abby Jane

That life works in seemingly strange ways is a given in most everyone's life. This "given," I have learned, also applies to death and the attempts we make at understanding the death of loved ones during the initial period of loss. Such is the case of our family and others close to our daughter Felicity Abby Jane, who was killed in a horrific head-on crash with a semi tractor-trailer on a country road in southern Minnesota February 1st, 2012. She was 27 years old when she died and had just begun her last two classes in completion of her bachelor's degree.

******

*Having completed the studies and satisfied the requirements prescribed by the Board of Directors of Walden University, Felicity Abby Jane Mathieu is conferred the degree of Bachelor of Science in Interdisciplinary Studies Cum Laude and to all rights, privileges and honors pertaining thereto.* – Paula Singer, Chair of the Board of Directors (awarded posthumously, August 25th, 2012)

\*\*\*\*\*\*

At the time of this writing, our grief is massive and, I suspect, will always be. It is, perhaps, much too early to reflect with great meaning or insight on her death, the accident, her funeral, the shared early shock, or the shared disbelief. I felt the need, however, to share some teachings learned, but not well understood, over 35 years ago before I lose their impact on my thinking about Felicity's death. These teachings were derived from conversations with two Lakota medicine men (*pejuta wicasa*), Sidney Keith and Martin High Bear, on the Cheyenne River Reservation in South Dakota in the mid-1970s.

Through a series of unusual circumstances, I had the great fortune to learn the language of the Lakota people as a young man and through continued studies during college. Later, as an assistant professor in the Center of Indian Studies at Black Hills State University, I began teaching Lakota language courses, which I continued doing for a dozen years or so at the university, as well as another college in eastern South Dakota, Dakota Wesleyan University. This effort led to a depth of opportunity to learn about the Lakota not often experienced by non-Indians and non-speakers. As a speaker of Lakota, in the community, I was not viewed as a simple *wasicu* or even as an *ieska*; a non-Lakota-speaking tribal member. Knowledge of the language opened many doors to accessing sacred knowledge, private knowledge, and the importance of understanding culture through language. Though unplanned, I was most fortunate to have had this aspect of my life develop in this manner.

Sometimes being a lifelong educator and experiencing all of the motivations for wanting to stand in front of a class narcissistically posing as a worship-worthy font of knowledge undermines one's real feelings at critical times. Such was the case four days after the death of our daughter as I prepared my eulogy for the funeral. What should have been full of memories and celebrations, as in the memorable eulogy prepared by my wife, turned into another opportunity for me to teach and attempt to elevate myself as the wise old professor thinking of the accolades I would receive. Perhaps this is being too hard on myself and only of limited truth, but some of these feelings were indeed present. I am not proud of that portion of my feelings at that time and experience considerable guilt at the shallowness I demonstrated, even if known only to me.

On the other hand, if one does not worry about the above self-revelations, there remains no question that my mind returned to Lakota spirituality as my wife and I as well as our two older sons sought some explanation of why

Felicity's death had occurred in both practical and philosophical terms. Should we have done something different that might have voided this accident? Who was at fault? What did we do wrong? Why did she choose to live in a rural area with dangerous roads? How could this happen? Was she or were we being punished? What was the role of God in this tragedy? Was it really true our beautiful daughter was dead? I am certain all parents, siblings, children, and others close to the deceased ask these same questions for which there are no answers, explanations, or rationale.

This experience of not being able to understand why reminded me of the teachings of Sidney Keith and Martin High Bear. In the end, it was the question why and how they would have responded that found its way into my eulogy for Felicity. In the months since that time, my time thinking about their likely response, based on their teachings, has moved me to a place of greater understanding both of Lakota spirituality and the death of Felicity.

What follows, then, is not text on our daughter; it is about what I have come to understand about Lakota spirituality inspired by the event of her death. These unconfirmed understandings are derived from what I believe I learned from Sidney and Martin. I say unconfirmed understandings because these two men are no longer alive for me to ask. I know in my heart, however, that they would both have said my understanding is alright. *Hecetu yelo*. That's enough for me.

# Part Two: The Learning Begins

**Sidney Keith and Martin High Bear**

When I was a much younger man and teaching full-time in the Center of Indian Studies at Black Hills State College, I had the opportunity to participate in community programs through the South Dakota Humanities Council. The majority of the programs were one-evening events organized by the Council and local community leaders. The purpose of the programs was to address social, political, or economic issues of importance to the community. As a representative from the state humanities council, my role was to address the particular issue from the perspective of the humanities. More specifically, my task was to reflect on how might a particular humanities discipline assist the community in thinking about the issue-that is, identifying the priorities, the culture, and the "character" of the community in relation to the issue facing the community. When I was included in such programs, my role was to assist in seeing if the language, culture, and history of the Lakota and other tribes may contribute to understanding a local issue whether or not the issue actually involved tribal matters or tribal people.

I met Sidney Keith (*Naca Cikala* – Little Chief) at Eagle Butte when planning a series of such programs on the Cheyenne River reservation. The issue at hand was an important piece of federal legislation that had recently been approved by Congress, titled the American Indian Self-Determination and Educational Assistance Act (Public Law 93-638) of 1976. The importance of the legislation was that, fundamentally, it permitted considerably greater local tribal control over Bureau of Indian Affairs (BIA) programs and schools on the reservations through local community boards with considerable authority for decision-making.  This legislation, in the intervening years, has changed the face of and nature of federal involvement in tribal affairs to the benefit of tribal members. At the time (1977), tribal members and local non-Indian residents of the reservations had little or no knowledge of Public Law 93-638. Only tribal leaders were aware of the existence and importance of the legislation. It was this community need that brought a non-Indian professor from Northern State College, Sidney Keith, Martin High Bear, and me together for two weeks in the summer of 1978 to offer the program in ten outlying communities in the districts of Cheyenne River.

Although I taught Lakota language at Black Hills State, Sidney served as translator so I could concentrate on program content as well as some translating for the other professor. Sidney's role also included helping us understand the character of each unique community and guidance on how to "nuance" the program for the particular community.

At that time, Sidney worked at the Indian Public Health Service hospital in Eagle Butte, as did

Martin High Bear, as I recall. Both Sidney and Martin were established medicine men in the reservation communities of Cheyenne River and were also well known and respected in Lakota communities, both on and off the reservation, all over South Dakota and beyond. Sidney had graciously offered his assistance for these programs that summer. His importance to the success of the programs was huge, and his willingness to discuss Lakota medicine and spirituality (religion) with me was of tremendous significance to me personally.

Like Martin, Sidney was a highly respected man in the Eagle Butte community as well as reservation-wide. Known for his work as a medicine man and someone very concerned about the passage of traditional ways, he wrote a small dictionary of the Lakota language for the Sioux Nation Arts Council based in Eagle Butte. The dictionary included translations needed at the hospital for the benefit of older Lakotas on the reservation.

Sidney took the anomaly of discussing his beliefs with a young white man who happened to speak Lakota and talk about tribal law in stride. Our conversations were genuine and deeply meaningful to me. He realized that he could share what he knew with me with the small hope that I really understood what he was saying. I heard and remembered what he told me, but Sidney was correct in knowing that it was not yet meaningful to me in the deepest sense.

Our time together was too short, but he made it count by telling me of his vision quest (*hanbleciya*), how it had affected his life, and what he now knew because of the direction and directions it had revealed. Much of it was difficult for a good Catholic boy from Minnesota to grasp, but I listened. Having participated in some ceremonial aspects of Lakota belief, such as sweat lodge (*inipi*) and prayer ceremonies (*lowanpi*), not all was lost on me. It was clear, however, that prior to visiting with Sidney, my previous experience and learning was only preliminary. There was so much more to Lakota belief. Additionally, I had not yet experienced the application of these beliefs and practices. I did not have to wait long.

## Part Three: Green Grass, 1977

### The Learning Encounters Belief

One of communities in which we were scheduled to offer our program on the American Indian Self-Determination Act was a small community situated on the Little Moreau River called Thunder Butte. On the day we were to present, Sidney's contact in the community informed us that there had been a death in the community the previous day. Because the Thunder Butte residents would be assisting the family of the deceased that evening, we would have to cancel our program.

Sidney reminded us that the next day, we were to travel to Green Grass; the most important community on the Cheyenne River reservation culturally. He suggested that we use the evening-off in our schedule to hold a *lowanpi* to pray to Sidney's spiritual contact for assistance in ensuring a good program at Green Grass.

Green Grass is the community where the sacred pipe brought by White Buffalo Calf Woman (*Ptejincala Ska Winyan*), in the sacred history of the Lakota, is kept (see map below). Stanley Looking Horse was, at the time, the pipe keeper (*Canunpa Wakan Kiciyuha*) and the Looking Horse family was prominent in the community of Green Grass as well as the entire Lakota nation. The Lakotas erected a structure for the pipe to protect it from loss, vandalism, or theft. With great care and reverence, Stanley Looking Horse and tribal members would unwrap the pipe of its protective wrappings and bundle at least annually or as the keeper needed it for tribal purposes. The pipe is inspected, rewrapped, and replaced in the structure. The keeper accompanies the pipe wherever it is brought if it must leave Green Grass.

Sidney and Martin High Bear conducted the *lowanpi* for our group and a few others that evening in Eagle Butte. The *lowanpi*, which means literally "they sing", is a prayer ceremony used when good results in some aspect of life are requested for an individual or community. As with *inipi* (for purification), yuwipi *(for* healing), and other ceremonies where the presence of the medicine man's spirit helper was needed, the room or lodge is made completely dark.

The medicine man sings intensively, requesting the spirit helper to come and hear the request for help. The spirit or spirits (*wanagi)* come and can be seen as small whitish-blue flashes in the room and all around the participants. Martin High Bear addressed the role of the singer in the ceremony, with Sidney leading and using his spiritual contact to pray to for help in making the program at Green Grass the following evening successful and meaningful. The impact of Sidney's spirit helper in hearing our prayers was certainly evident the next evening.

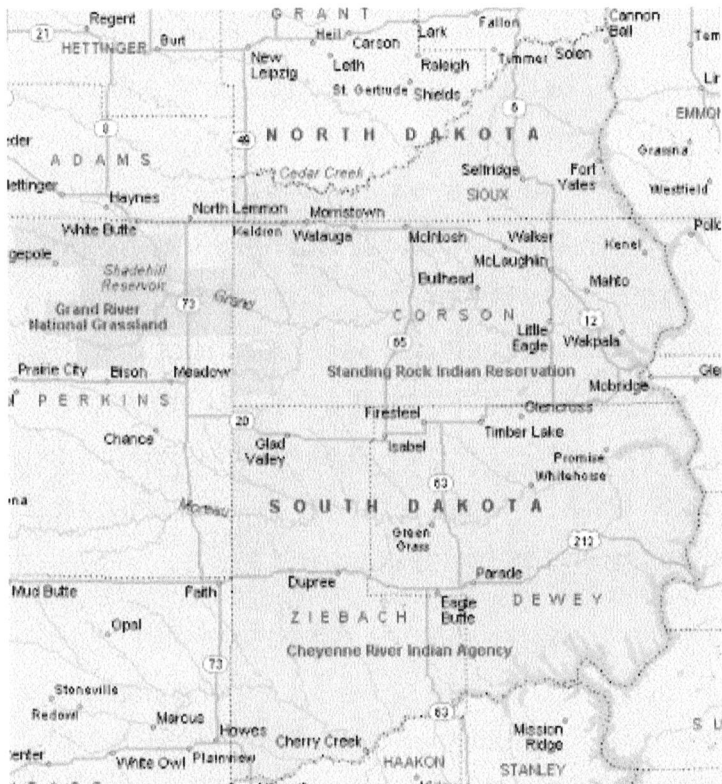

The Cheyenne River Reservation is home to four tribes of the seven tribes of the seven council fires: Sihasapa (Blackfeet), Miniconjou (Plant near the Water), Itazipco (Sans Arc or Without Bows), Oohenumpa (Two Kettle)
Source: Wowapi .com

A dirt road took us to Green Grass and we arrived at the Green Grass community's meeting building about 5:00 pm in a 61 Ford

Falcon. The community building was a fairly
worn out and unpainted wood frame building.
Most of the window frames lacked glass,
although many had window-size cloth curtains.
The area surrounding the building and in front
for parking was hard dirt. Two outhouses or
shelters constructed of split lengths of
corrugated metal drainage culverts stood on
end and were dug into the ground deep enough
to be solid. The open side of the culverts faced
away from the building.

The valley surrounding the site was one of the
most beautiful I can recall. Up all of the gradual
hillsides around us was prairie tall grass made
golden by the sun low in the sky. In groups of
three, four, and five, horses grazed on the
hillsides half hidden by the tall grass. One
certainly could see the relationship of the
presence of the sacred pipe to the subtle but
powerful setting. To the west, a bank of dark
blue thunder clouds provided great contrast to
the gold of the grass. Although beautiful, it

seemed certain that some serious weather was approaching.

We were met by Stanley Looking Horse's wife in the kitchen area of the building. She was preparing the usual, but very much appreciated, traditional meal of *wojapi* (a thickened chokecherry sauce)*, wigli un kagapi (*fry bread- literally "they make in grease"), and *talo wahanpi (*unthickened beef and root-vegetable stew). As we began to set up for the program and arranged the metal folding chairs already in the building, community members from Green Grass began to arrive. Sidney and I chatted with folks casually until it looked like all that were attending were present. The program progressed as usual with a few questions, some confusion about "self-determination" as distinguished from "termination" policy of the 1950s, and some additional clarification of the tribe's and community's role in local control through contract which was introduced in the new legislation.

As some of these issues were being clarified in the discussion, an awesome and howling blast of wind (*tateyanpa*) suddenly hit the building. The short curtains covering some of the window frames were blown in perpendicular from the walls. The sound of the wind and the curtain cloth snapping in the wind made it impossible to continue the program, so we waited 10 minutes or so until the wind tapered slowly back to normal. Although it earned no comment that I recall from the group, the presence of the wind was not accompanied by the other expected elements of the storm we saw when we arrived. There was no lightning, no thunder, and no rain. There was just the wind, and it left no damage of which we were aware.

When the curtains returned to their original positions against the walls, we concluded the program and responded to final questions and comments. The members of the audience began to leave the building, with some staying to visit briefly or bring their *wateca* buckets to Mrs. Looking Horse for some leftovers to bring home. We stayed to assist with cleanup of the kitchen area and loaded our stuff into the old Ford Falcon. The ground around the building looked the same as when we arrived - dry. There was no evidence of any weather having occurred that evening other than the wind we experienced while inside the building.

Our perceptions changed, however, as soon as we left the building grounds for we discovered that the dirt road had turned into a Cheyenne River quagmire known as "gumbo" from a heavy dose of rain from the storm.

******

*It was said that the most popular local dance band in central South Dakota was the Gumbo Combo.*

******

The Falcon was barely able to navigate the mud which clung to the tires. The trip back to Eagle

Butte took well over twice as long as the trip to Green Grass and was characterized by consistent mud, downed tree branches, and other storm-related hazards.  When we returned to the Wheel-Inn Motel in Eagle Butte, the owner said that they had been hit with a severe thunderstorm not only in Eagle Butte, but most everywhere on and off of the reservation. It appeared, to no surprise to Martin and Sidney, that the 30 yard radius around the community building in Green Grass was the only earth left dry anywhere in the reservation and the region.  I remain convinced today of the efficacy of the *Iowanpi*  the previous evening in protecting the Green Grass community members who ventured out to attend our program at the community building just as had been requested of Sidney's spiritual contact.

It was in this context, along with my studies, my knowledge of Lakota language, and the milieu of my world at the time, over the next few days and later, I sought further insight into what I had experienced that evening in Green Grass on the Cheyenne River reservation. Primarily Sidney, but also Martin, provided straight-forward descriptions and an amazing amount of patience. It was clear that they believed the occurrence would happen just the way it did and had been told such by their spiritual helpers the previous evening in Eagle Butte.

# Part Four: Misinterpreting the Lakota and Worldview of Others

**(Of which, of course, this may very well be just another example.....)**

Before moving into a discussion of the beliefs of the Lakota, especially as viewed from the outside, some background information is necessary as well as some perspectives about attempting to understand another culture. Any understanding of Lakota belief and understanding of spirituality must take into account the context in which the Lakota lived prior to significant white contact, the environment of the prairie and plains, and the fragility of life in a subsistence economy. This understanding is not for the purpose of limiting the efficacy of Lakota belief to such environments but rather to help explain the beliefs held by the Lakota and the role they played in the lives of individuals and the community.

Lakota presence on the prairie and plains of what is now southwestern Minnesota, southern North Dakota, South Dakota, northern Nebraska, and eastern Montana and Wyoming came about following the pressure and conflict with the Anishinabe as they moved into the woodland areas of the western Great Lakes and northern Minnesota and Wisconsin. A major battle ensued around 1700 between the Sioux nations and the Anishinabe near Lake Mille Lacs in Minnesota in which the Sioux were defeated.

Of the major nations of the Sioux, the Dakota occupied the true prairies of Minnesota while the Nakota settled in the areas where the prairies mixed with the plains of the eastern Dakotas bounded largely by the Missouri River. The Lakotas settled on the high plains of South Dakota, Nebraska, and eastern Wyoming, where the roughly simultaneous introduction of the horse from tribes to the south permitted a good life. A smaller group of Sioux people speaking

Jakota (Assiniboine) settled in Northeast Montana.

As the environment changes from one area to the next, so do the beliefs reflected in the vocabulary within the language often change. These differences between Dakota, Nakota, Lakota, and Jakota strongly suggest the fundamental importance of the environment to which the tribes responded.

For the Lakota, even with the stability and richness of life permitted by the presence of the horse compared to life prior to horses, the climate they faced made life itself a huge and constant challenge. The extremes of heat and cold, relative barrenness of the land, and distance in a hunting and gathering economy created an often fragile line between life and death. This fragility was manifest in all aspects of spiritual and non-spiritual life.

The result is a Lakota world view where survival cannot be taken for granted and where a complex understanding and close observation of the environment as well as a clear understanding of the role of spirituality in life is present at all times.

As an outcome of this environmental understanding, the Lakota paid great attention to the often seemingly unimportant subtleties of the landscape and changes that mark the passing of time and the significance of the changes such as those revealed in names of the periods of time from one new moon to the next. These names change somewhat from reservation to reservation as what is notable in each environment changes.

******

*Wiotehika wi*:  Hard moon

*Cannapopa wi*:  Moon when the trees "pop"

*Siyo Istohcapi wi*:  Moon when the prairie chicken's eyes freeze

*Wihakaktacepapi wi*:  Moon when the youngest wife breaks bones for the marrow fat.

*Canwapeto wi*:  Moon when the leaves turn green.

*Wipazutkan Waste wi:*  Moon when the June berries are good.

*Canpasapa wi:*  Moon when the chokecherries are black.

*Wasuton wi:*  Moon when things ripen.

*Canwapegi wi*:  Moon when the leaves turn brown.

*Canwapekasna wi:*  Moon when the leaves are blown off the trees.

*Takiyuha wi:*  Moon when deer mate.

*Tahecapsun wi:*  Moon when deer shed their antlers.

******

## Language and Cultural Insight

A primary rationale for studying a second language is the cultural understanding one achieves concerning the target language's people and, perhaps more importantly, a deeper understanding of one's own. The fundamental relationship of language to culture has caused some linguists to ask which came first; did the culture developed reflect the environment in which the speakers found themselves and the language was developed to describe that culture? Or, as some suggest, did the language develop first to describe the environment and then did the language that determined the culture (Sapir and Whorf, 1962)? In any event, it is clear that the two cannot be considered independent: language and culture are inextricably and fundamentally linked. Additionally, as one's environment changes, it is clear that the language and culture will also change.

Some examples that portray the linkage between language and culture are important to illustrate the idea. Let me begin with an example from Spanish contrasted with the same example from English (Fernandez, 1968). Imagine you are leaving on a trip to a desirable location and have arrived at the airport. You proceed to the gate of departure and, to your great surprise, the door to the ramp is closed and the plane is pulling away from the gate. The gate agent informs you that you cannot board and will have to schedule another flight. After the first words out of your mouth (something like "%@*&#^$" or "darn"), an English-speaking traveler might say, "*I missed the plane.*" A fellow Spanish-speaking traveler, however, might say, "*El avion me dejo.*" meaning *the plane has left me*. Although the difference is subtle, it may offer an insight into the world-view of the two different cultures represented in this example.

As both English and Spanish have a basic sentence grammar of subject – verb – object, we can surmise that in English, the traveler (I) is the subject of the sentence and the plane is the direct object. In this grammar, the subject of the sentence carries the responsibility for the action or "fault." Implied is that the English-speaking traveler was responsible for not arriving in time to board the plane. Implied also is that the traveler could have affected the result by doing something different to assure they were able to board on time. Control, then, of the situation was in the hands of the traveler.

In the Spanish example, your sentence describing your situation has the plane as the subject and you are the direct object. Implied here is that it was the plane's "fault" that you were unable to board. As the direct object of the sentence, there was basically nothing you could do to have changed the situation. In a sense, it was "fate" that you would did not board the plane. It was meant to be.

Although one must be careful in drawing conclusions from an example or two, it could be said that the switch from English to Spanish of who was responsible, indicates a fundamental cultural difference with respect to notions of fate or destiny versus self-determination and control.

As with any two languages, the Lakota language provides many opportunities for misinterpretation when the language is removed from its context. Thus, misinterpretations can be derived from loose or popular and translations, misinterpreting an action, or outcome in the context of one's own cultural and linguistic understanding.

******

*(In a discussion with Sinte Gleska University Lakota language instructor, Doris Leader Charge, about Lakota verb tenses, I was advised........)*

*David, you have translated Lakota verb tense forms as past, present, and future in the textbook you are writing. These translations are not correct although probably they are often understood this way.*

*Notice that your past and present tense use the same verb forms. They cannot be used to describe what has happened or is happening in the present. They are the same thing. What you have taken "kte" to mean as a future tense marker in sentences is also incorrect.  Think of a common phrase using kte in another context. Winyan kte or Winkte means "not real woman" or homosexual. This use of kte is the real meaning when used in association with a verb. There are only two "tenses" in Lakota, and neither refers directly to time. What you have translated as past and present are only one tense and it means "real". Kte following a verb means it is "unreal". Thus, the first tense in Lakota include those actions that are real because they have already occurred or they are occurring now. Both can be seen or have been seen. The second tense describes things that are unreal because they have not occurred and cannot be seen. – Doris Leader Charge*

\*\*\*\*\*\*

For a long time, I have wrestled with trying to be sure that what I thought was true and what I thought important in my teaching did not slip into mere translations of words or cultural artifacts that reflected no insight into the worldview of the Lakota. It is a daunting task as it often relies on native intervention when mistakes are made, but such intervention is becoming increasingly rare as the number of Lakota speakers decreases. As one can see, the

loss of a language is, indeed, the loss of a
culture.

# Part Five: Lakota Cosmogony and Spirituality

## The Nature of Sacred and Non-Sacred Narratives

The sacred, however it might be defined from one people to the next or even each individual to the next, serves many purposes that appear universal in all religious traditions. All societies, it seems, need to have a notion of what is sacred and, in their own context, all are correct and appropriate. All are based on literatures, texts, and experiences held in common that may be written or solely oral or both. The extent to which elements of each are believed are often as much a function of their purpose as well as individual or community belief. Lakota spirituality and Lakota People provide no exception to this observation.

In Lakota, there are several types of sacred narrative literatures that derive from oral tradition (*oyake*, act of narration). At the level of cosmogony, an expansive set of sacred tradition answers questions about the origin of the Lakota world, the Lakota people, and how various elements in this world came to be (*ehanni oyake*, long-ago stories). Spirits are identified in association with all natural phenomena such as thunder, lightning, rain, and important animal and plant resources such as buffalo and choke cherries. The Lakota cosmogony is as complex and comprehensive as that of any society and limited only by the nature of oralcy, if at all. At this level, it may be safe to say that no single individual knew the entire literature, but at the *tiospaye* (band or community), perhaps, and tribal levels, the literature was complete. Thus, such sacred knowledge was the domain not of individuals, but certain elders, medicine men and women, and specified members of military societies whose origins are linked to that of the larger tribe and can be relied upon to recall, at least in part, the cosmogony of the people.

There is no question that this narrative literature (*ehanni oyake*) was and is meant to be believed as the literature describe how things and the people came to be. There is another set of stories (*wowicake wicooyake*), also meant to be believed, that exists for more practical purposes in carrying out the sacred practices and events of Lakota spirituality as well as the "tribally-remembered past" (as opposed to narratives of individuals). In Lakota, much of this revolves around how things "used to be" at some time in the past such as before having horses or while living in an earlier period of time or place. These narratives are unconcerned about when they occurred. It is only important to know that they happened long ago before anyone now living remembered.

The most important among these is the story of the sacred pipe and the bringing of the pipe to the Lakota by *Ptejincala Ska Winyan* (White Buffalo Calf Woman). It is this pipe that is kept at Green Grass and kept by the Looking Horse family. The use of the sacred pipe is defined by the seven rites of the pipe that the people were given by *Ptejincala Ska Winyan*. These rites mark the important universal events of life in which the sacred pipe plays the important role of communication with the sacred world. The story of *Ptejincala Ska Winyan* is undoubtedly the most sacred of stories in providing the "how to do it" aspects of Lakota spirituality. All Lakotas would be expected to know this story well. A pantheon of other stories exists in the literature of the Lakota that have spiritual aspects or involve spiritual characters, yet are not meant to be believed (*ohunkanka woyake*). These stories are for the purposes of teaching, by way of example, proper behavior, the wisdom behind important decisions faced by individuals, and the consequences of poor decision-making and behavior. Among these are the *Iktomi* (spider) stories, similar to other trickster characters in other societies. Children would be told the *Iktomi* stories often and reminded of proper behavior as necessary through the retelling. The stories provide a fundamental moral education that expresses the values of the people and how they are applied in life situations.

******

*Iktomi was going along when he came upon a group of young women and their infant children. They were looking to the west and talking about how red the sky in the west was. When they saw Iktomi, they asked why the sky was so red. Iktomi, seeing the little babies, said, "The sky is made red by the red chokecherries over there." He continued, "You all should go there with your baskets and pick as many berries as you can because there are very good to eat right now. I will watch your babies while you are gone." The young women left to find the chokecherries but there were none. They returned to where Iktomi was watching their babies. They found, however, that Iktomi had eaten their babies and was gone. His story had been a trick. They cried over the loss of their children and how foolish they had been.*
– Kate Blue Thunder in *Buckskin Tokens*

******

Additionally, another set of stories includes the remembered histories of the Lakota and may also describe spiritual ideas and events. These include the retelling of dreams, one's *hanbleciya* (vision quest), and other spiritual encounters. Good examples of these are those told by Sidney Keith to his son-in-law, Melvin Miner, in *A Common Man* (Thomas, 2009). These stories are also meant to be believed by the listener as they are believed by the teller.

To Sidney, the importance of the sacred literatures surrounding the origin of the people, how things came to be, and such lie in the ability to answer the complex questions that all people and tribes ask about themselves.

\*\*\*\*\*\*

*You know, everything had to begin, and this is how it was; the Kiowa came one by one into the world through a hollow log. They were many more than now, but not all of them got out. There was a woman whose body was swollen up with child, and she got stuck in the log. After that, no one could get through, and that is why the*

*Kiowa are a small tribe in number. They looked around and saw the new world. It made them glad to see so many things. They called themselves Kwuda, "coming out."* - N. Scott Momaday in *Way to Rainy Mountain*

\*\*\*\*\*\*

The answers, however, are not particularly important in understanding the group's or individual's relationship to the supernatural world. In the Lakota world, what is important are the understandings that are derived from observation of the natural world, things revealed in *hanbleciya*, insights revealed in dreams, and knowledge obtained often with the help of medicine men. Further, the sacred literature describing Lakota cosmogony is not particularly instructive about how to live, relationships with family, *tiospaye*, tribe, or how to seek spiritual help. The sacred literatures generally do not provide mandates for behavior, what people should believe in order to attain a desirable afterlife, or confirmation of the existence of God or gods. Sidney suggested to me that it is simply all *Wakan* and we try to understand it the best we can.

# Part Six: God and Gods

## Tunkasila, Wakan Tanka

In traditional Lakota belief, a supreme being or "god," as a representable character, is not present. *Wakan Tanka*, Great Mystery, is often interpreted as literally meaning the Great Spirit. While an understandable translation, it leads the uninformed to think that the concept of God as we know the idea in the Western tradition also exists in Lakota belief. The appeal that this idea has is evidenced by the popularity of its usage. Non-Indians, non-Lakota tribal people and many Lakotas themselves, particularly younger Lakotas who are also non-speakers of Lakota, often use *Wakan Tanka* and/or *Tunkasila* (Grandfather) in a manner similar to how the notion of God is used in Christianity. The idea of *Wakan Tanka* as God, probably because of its simplicity, has become so fundamental with regard to American Indian spirituality that it is now being taught to Lakota youth as the actual meaning of the word and the concept in what they now regard as traditional belief. The tragedy is that, with the practical death of the Lakota language at some time in the future, the linguistic and cultural complexity of *Wakan Tanka* will be lost in favor of the simpler and more understandable idea. Events such as this are the result whenever a language is lost to the world-- a phenomenon linguists estimate occurs many, many times each year all over the world.

In contrast to the popular meaning, the actual meaning of the term *Wakan Tanka* is great or big (*tanka*) mystery or mysterious (*Wakan*). Thus, the traditional use of the term does not refer to a definable being. Rather, it describes Lakota understanding of the supernatural or spiritual world. In a manner of speaking, in traditional Lakota belief, it would be presumptuous for Lakotas to believe they could understand the non-worldly parts of life when, indeed, they could not. Thus, the concept of

*Wakan* refers to those things and matters that could not be understood by humankind. The spiritual "world," then, could only be described as *Wakan* or a mystery. The same idea was extended to material things that were not easily understood. Perhaps the best example being the horse. When first witnessed by the Lakota, the horse was termed *sunkawakan* (mysterious dog), referring to the only domesticated animal existing to the Lakota. This new animal was indeed mysterious initially, but the term stayed in the vocabulary even after the horse was fully incorporated into the culture. Other items from the Europeans were also best understood as mysterious such as the gun (*mazawakan*; mysterious metal) or liquor (*mniwakan*; mysterious water). Natural places with unusual qualities were also referred to as mysterious such as Spirit Lake (*Mdewakan*; mysterious lake in the Dakota language) in Minnesota, which "bubbles" from an underground spring. The importance of the above ideas in addressing the concept of *Wakan* will be more apparent later.

It is clear, however, that words indicating what appear to be discrete characters in Lakota belief are used by traditional Lakotas, including medicine men such as Sidney Keith and Martin High Bear.  In a prayer or description in a public venue or a prayer in ceremonies such as *inipi* (sweat lodge/purification), *lowanpi*  (singing prayers), and *yuwipi* (healing), a medicine man or woman will address the prayer to "grandfather," "mother earth,"  the spirits of the directions, lightning, or thunder.  Again, this does not infer the concept of a discrete god of all things or gods of particular phenomena, but rather a name that refers to how one might "think" about the mysteries that exist. When applied to real situations and needs, it is helpful to individuals to label that part of the mystery by name.  When using the word *tunkasila*, then, in a prayer or lesson, the medicine man is really referring to the broad notion of the world and things that cannot be understood by the Lakotas.

\*\*\*\*\*\*

*"See, I fill this sacred pipe with the bark of the red willow; but before we smoke it, you must see how it is made and what it means. These four ribbons hanging here on the stem are the four quarters of the universe. The black one is for the west where the thunder beings live to send us rain; the white one for the north, whence comes the great white cleansing wind; the red one for the east, whence springs the light and where the morning star lives to give men wisdom; the yellow for the south whence come the summer and the power to grow."*

*But these four spirits are only one spirit after all, and this eagle feather here is for that one, which is like a father, and also it is for the thoughts of men that should rise high as eagles do. Is not the sky a father and the earth a mother, and are not all living things with feet or wings or roots their children? . . . And because it means all this, and more than any man can understand, the pipe is holy."* - Black Elk in *Black Elk Speaks*

\*\*\*\*\*\*

In <u>Black Elk Speaks</u> – author John Niehardt is told by Black Elk of the vision he had when was a young man and seriously ill with an unspecified disease. In the vision, Black Elk refers to the horses of the directions with north, east, west, and south by the types of horses he sees along with other beings and natural phenomena. At the same time, however, he acknowledges that they are all one thing and that is *Wakan*.

\*\*\*\*\*\*

*Then I was standing on the highest mountain of them all, and round about beneath was the whole hoop of the world. And while I stood there I saw more than I can tell and I understood more than I saw; for I was seeing in a sacred manner the shape of all things in the spirit and the shape of all shapes as they must live together as one being. And I saw that it was holy.* – Black Elk in *Black Elk Speaks*

\*\*\*\*\*\*

The notion of the "hoop" of the world described by Black Elk and others describes accurately the horizon which can be seen in all directions when viewed from a high location. Bear Butte (*Mato*

*Paha*), near Sturgis, South Dakota, is such a place. I often spent time there alone or with my family enjoying its singular beauty, but also the beauty and understanding revealed when the details of objects, natural and man-made, can no longer be seen. The height and the distance render all into a myriad of colors and ill-defined shapes that blend into each other and make the unity of all things more clear.

******

*You can't explain it except by going to the circles within circles idea, the spirit splitting itself up into stones, trees, tiny insects even, making them all Wakan by his everpresence. And in turn all these myriad of things which make up the universe flowing back to their source, united in the one Grandfather spirit.*
– Lame Deer

******

In a manner similar to the use of discrete entities when really addressing the unknown, Lakota belief makes reference to places of importance. The physical world known to the Lakotas was termed *makoce* and the land inhabited by spiritual entities was termed *wanagiyata*. Everything in *wanagiyata,* the land of the spirits, was *Wakan.* And, in the recorded beliefs of the medicine men, everything in the physical world was also *Wakan*. Thus, *Wakan* is everything and is such because it is either intrinsically unknowable or it has become *Wakan* because of *ton*, the endowment of spiritual quality that makes something (or someone) *Wakan*.

# Part Seven: Communicating with the Wakan

Even though Lakotas knew that the *wanagiyata* and the *Wakan* were concepts not to be understood by humans, spiritual intervention into the lives of ordinary people was believed to be possible. This could be done in differing, but related ways. First, recall that *Ptejincala Ska Winyan* brought the Lakotas the sacred pipe and taught the people how to use it. In addition to how the pipe should be properly handled ceremonially, she introduced the ceremonies or rites of the sacred pipe which offered protocols for the human needs addressed. It was through the use of the pipe that the people, via the medicine man, could communicate with the *Wakan*. Imagine the sweet-smelling smoke of the sacred pipe rising and slowly disappearing as one prayed or in other ways communicated with the world and entities beyond one's understanding. The pipe was a very powerful tool to bring one's requests, needs, and aspirations to the attention of *Wakan Tanka*.

******

*"....and there around the big tepee they waited for the sacred woman (White Buffalo Calf Woman). And after a while she came, very beautiful and singing, and as she went into the tepee this is what she sang:*

> *With visible breath I am walking. A voice I am sending as I walk. In a sacred manner I am walking. With visible tracks I am walking. In a sacred manner I walk.*

*And as she sang, there came from her mouth a white cloud that was good to smell.* — Little Wound in *Lakota Belief and Ritual*

******

*Ptejincala Ska Winyan* also revealed seven rites which showed how to use the pipe in communicating with Wakan for certain purposes. The seven rites of the sacred pipe included, Keeping of the Spirit (*Wanagi Kiciyuha*), Purification (*Inipi - literally, "they* sweat"), Crying for a Vision (*Hanblechiyapi*), Sun Dance (*Wiwanyan Wacipi*), Making of Relatives (*Hunkapi*), Preparing a Girl for Womanhood (*Isna Ta Awi Ca Lowan*), Throwing of the Ball (*Tapa Wanka Yan*).

A second and related tool for communicating to the *Wakan* was through the assistance of a *pejuta wicasa* (medicine man). Medicine men, such as Sidney and Martin, were individuals of the tribe who attempted and completed the *hanbleciya* or vision quest as well as additional tasks and learning under the tutelage of another medicine man. Sometimes encouraged by others, particularly a medicine man, or seemingly spiritually chosen, an individual worked with a medicine man to prepare for the vision quest. With such help, the individual chose a time to begin and location. The location chosen for the vision quest was extremely important. The site was best if at a high point geographically, isolated, and accessible to a variety of spiritual helpers who would naturally inhabit the site chosen. Selecting a location that was the highest point in the area allowed the individual to see what Black Elk termed-- "the whole hoop of the world" while he experienced his vision.

When the appointed time arrived, the individual would go to the selected location of isolation and fast and pray until such time as a spiritual helper revealed itself to the individual. The helper may take the form of an animal, bird, tree, reptile, even inanimate objects occasionally. During the *hanbleciya*, the seeker opened himself up to close observation of everything experienced, the presence of potential spiritual helpers who may attempt communication with the seeker.

Following the *hanbleciya* and further tutelage, the individual may begin to call upon the spiritual helper for access and assistance of the great mystery's potential for insight into the needs of the individual, the individual being assisted, or the community requiring assistance.

The request for assistance occurs in the context of Lakota ceremonies and the presence of the pipe. During ceremonies using the pipe in communication with the *Wakan*, such as *inipi, lowanpi, and yuwipi,* smoking the pipe assists in sending the prayer of the medicine man to his spiritual helper requesting understanding, help, or intervention. The helper will inform the medicine man of the helper's presence via physical contact, whispered communication, or other spiritual means.

\*\*\*\*\*\*

*I remember sitting next to Monica Garreau during a lowanpi when she whispered to me, "All of a sudden there was a deer hoof in my hand and I am sure it was alive."* - David Mathieu

\*\*\*\*\*\*

The presence of the medicine man's spiritual helper indicates that the prayer has been heard. The helper will communicate the assistance or intervention provided to the medicine man or, on occasion to those assembled in the ceremony. It is not uncommon for some or all in the ceremony to receive a sign directly from the helper. All will experience the presence of the spirit(s) in the form of flashes of blue-white light occurring in the total darkness of the ceremony.

******

*We're not holy. We work with the Spirits. They are the ones that are holy, but we are the interpreter. They teach us, they tell us and then we pass this on to you. Without them we can't do all these things. So our egos shouldn't be real powerful. We realize that somebody gave us this power to use for the people. They gave it to us, they could take it back. It's more powerful, more meaningful when we help people, not our self, but to help the people. We are here to help our future generations, especially when it deals with health or for a better life.* - Sidney Keith

******

# Part Eight: Understanding *Wakan*

## *Wakan* as Mystery and a Spiritual Position

Conceptually, *Wakan* is a seemingly simple notion as its meaning implies. Expressing the spiritual world as a big mystery would seem to be the end of the discussion, but there is more to apprehend. *Wakan* is, at its core, an ambiguous, yet very honest, explanation of why we cannot understand a reality we desperately wish we could. *Wakan*, then, is a spiritual "position," on which to base an understanding of one's spiritual and physical worlds as well as the relationship between the two.

******

*The sea lies all about us.... In its mysterious past it encompasses all the dim origins of life.* - Rachel Carson in an entry for mysterious in the *American Heritage Dictionary*

******

This perspective does not provide many answers, as Lakotas face a hostile environment and, occasionally, hostile neighbors. It does, however, introduce the idea that spirituality does not require certainty. Spirituality does not require prescribed answers. The seeking of spiritual intervention does not require standardized methodologies, deviance from which jeopardizes the efficacy of the intervention.

This is a crucial concept in coming to a greater understanding of the spiritual world. Rather than one's spirituality being based on a search for answers, cosmic or otherwise, and the commitment to a particular viewpoint or religious tradition, the Lakota world view would assume the inability of humans to understand or commit to a narrow understanding of the spiritual world. The real world of the Lakota was a complex mixture and array of natural phenomena, often dangerously scarce resources, occasional intertribal conflict over scarce resources, and a well understood notion of the need for balance in a world where the dividing line between life and death was a very fine one indeed.  It was also a line that could change reality quickly and not just for individuals, but for the entire community or *tiospaye* with whom one shared life and depended upon for the greater part of the year. *Wakan*, then, is clearly a spiritual position from which one can address the struggle of life and death.

****** **

**mys·te·ri·ous** ☒ *adj.*

**1.** *Of, relating to, or being a mystery: mysterious and infinite truths.*
**2.** *Simultaneously arousing wonder and inquisitiveness, and eluding explanation or comprehension: a mysterious visitor; mysterious conduct.* – entry in *American Heritage Dictionary*

******

This spiritual position of *Wakan* does, however, invite potentially new and alternative inquiry into the nature of events and, in general, how things work. Our Western perspective has little tolerance for this perspective, but it shows us the real importance of an event in the lives of the Lakota. Certainly, it is difficult to understand what real insight we have when we discover the cause for such an event. Lakotas see the question in relation to their own lives and a deepened understanding of the human relationship to *Wakan*. Not knowing, and believing one cannot "know," then, becomes useful to the real world lives of the Lakota -- not only out of humility and honesty, but also out of practicality. Approaching the idea of *Wakan* as spiritual insight sounds counterintuitive, but admitting lack of understanding is what permits Lakota the adaptability needed to survive as conditions and situations change.

******

*For us Lakotas, it is not important to know why the bird flies south. It is important to know the bird and its relationship to all that is in time and space. – Gerald*

*Clifford* in *"American Indian Studies as an Academic Discipline"*

\*\*\*\*\*\*

**Wakan as Balance:**

As alluded to above, Lakota spirituality focuses highly on the need to maintain "balance" in the real world as well as in the spiritual world. This balance is expressed in perceptions of correct and incorrect, good and bad, equality and inequality, and cultural "rules" to help ensure that the world remain in balance and address imbalance when it occurs.  Again, the existence of the *tiospaye* depends on a narrow fulcrum between survival and non-survival. The timely ability to find and harvest buffalo, antelope, and deer, the impact of winter cold and summer heat on access to water, to find gathered root vegetables, berries, and nuts, all depended on a stable and balanced world.

When events occurred that threatened this balance, the individual, the *tiospaye*, and the tribe had the task of returning the world to balance. Most commonly occurring events impacting balance were community violence, tribal conflict, and individual inappropriate actions that threatened community stability and/or the group's ability to secure food, fuel, and other resources as well as safety required for survival.

For example, following conflict with another tribe where a life may have been taken or significant injury was done, the Lakota needed to "debrief" and think about the occurrence in order to return to a non-violent or "normal" attitude and perspective. Other balancing occurred in response to actions of individuals within the community that threatened the community's well-being, such as conflict with another community member, not following the prescriptions of the *itancan* (headman) and the *wakicunza* (council) when the community needed to act as one, most often in the pursuit of buffalo or other wild game, with all individuals participating and individual roles fulfilled. Disregard for the fundamental interrelatedness of all things, actions, and relationships were not to be tolerated. Significant violations of this understanding must be atoned and could rise to individuals being banished from the *tiospaye*; an action that often led to death without the community. As a last example to this point is the often-made assertion that Lakotas actively give thanks to the spirits of animals, plants, and trees at the moment when taken for food, fuel, and shelter. While often exaggerated in media depicting tribal scenes, there is a spoken or unspoken belief that premature death, even when clearly occurring for the greater good has unbalanced the world. Some measure of atonement is necessary to restore balance.

Implicit in Lakota belief, then, is the nature of balance in *Wakan*. Although it represents that which cannot be understood in the world, *Wakan* is afforded some structure by humankind as they interact with their physical world. The need to insure the well-being of the community comes with a level of requisite individual behavior in order to remain a part of the community. As *Wakan* represents also the balance between the physical and non-physical worlds, human contributions to upsetting this balance must be addressed.

### *Wakan* as an Endowed Quality; *Ton*

A valid question at this point is that if *Wakan* is the unknowable dimension of the Lakota world, how is it that we hear of sacred things, people, and places such as the sacredness of the Black Hills and Bear Butte, Black Elk as a holy man, and sacred objects.

In Lakota, there is a word and concept, *ton* that explains the above. Within the idea of *Wakan*, there is nothing intrinsically sacred or holy other than the concept of *Wakan*. Because certain individuals such as medicine men, or places that are unique or are the sites of spiritual events, are associated with *Wakan* and, of themselves, are not to be understood or explained, *Wakan* becomes an endowed quality or "*ton.*" The Black Hills are indeed *Wakan* in their mystery, mysterious places, mysterious uniqueness as a landform amidst an unmountainous plain, and a place of mysterious abundance in comparison to the high plains. Because the Black Hills are *Wakan*, a mystery, they are attributed by humans to be thought of as sacred or holy rather than intrinsically such.

******

*Wakan was anything that was hard to understand. A rock was sometimes Wakan. Anything might be Wakan. When anyone did something that no one understood, this was Wakan. If the thing done was what no one could understand, it was Wakan Tanka. How the world was made is Wakan Tanka. How the sun was made is Wakan Tanka. How men used to talk to the animals and birds was Wakan Tanka. Where the spirits and ghosts are is Wakan Tanka. How the spirits act is Wakan. A spirit is Wakan.* - Good Seat in *Lakota Belief and Ritual*

\*\*\*\*\*\*

Our use of the terms "holy" and "sacred" to equate to Wakan as a quality of particular objects, places, and texts is what makes the concept of *Wakan* difficult to understand and misuse of the idea understandable outside of the context of the Lakota language. In English, it seems clear that certain things are <u>intrinsically</u> holy or sacred. Their "holiness" or "sacredness" is revealed and declared to be such by a particular religious community or organization. Certain relics, places, and individuals (such as saints) become sacred or holy and remain such in the view of the believers.

\*\*\*\*\*\*

*In getting ready for the Sun Dance, the medicine man in charge selects a good tree to be cut down and used as the sacred pole from which the Sun Dancers attach their piercings by long pieces of hide. The dancers dance away from the sacred pole until the piercing is torn from the skin of the dancer. When the Sun Dance is over after two or three days, the sacred pole is removed from the dance area and burned. The tree was wakan during the Sun Dance, but when finished, it returned to being just a tree. -* Martin High Bear

******

All things may be seen as potentially sacred and holy in the Lakota world view because they are *Wakan* and are all a part of the great mystery that we futilely seek to understand. Depending on context, individual things and people can be considered *Wakan* because of *ton*; their association with that which cannot be understood.

# Part Nine: Grieving and Wakan

## The Understanding Begins

Although we all experience the death of individuals we have come to know over the course of life or have been given to us by blood, marriage, friendships, and collegial relationships, what we <u>learn</u> about death comes slowly, but what we <u>understand</u> about death may come even more slowly. In some cases, however, both may come all too quickly.

\*\*\*\*\*\*

*February 1, 2012, 2:00pm. "Is this David Mathieu?" "Yes, it is." "This is Sergeant _____ calling from the State Highway Patrol in Rochester." Do you have a daughter by the name of Felicity Mathieu?" "Yes, I do. What's the problem?" "I can't tell you over the phone, but there has been an accident and there are two highway patrolmen waiting to speak with you at your home in Savage." "Oh no! Is this bad?" "Yes....., I am afraid it is."*

\*\*\*\*\*\*

I remember being alone with my father at his home in the early morning when he died. He had been bed-ridden for the previous three days and the in-home hospice nurse who visited several times told us the end was very near. Members of my family helped me with his physical needs during this time and I would stay overnight. He slept restlessly through much of this time and was largely incoherent when he awoke. At the end, as I was helping him attend to his bathroom needs, he sat upright on the edge of the bed and slumped backward for his final breath. I sat with him for about an hour crying, talking to him, and trying to absorb what had just occurred before contacting the authorities and my family.

I'm not sure of all of my feelings at the time, but there was a profound sadness while I tried to understand the event of my father's death in terms of what I believed or did not believe. In the end, I think I understood that I simply did not understand.

In the case of the death of our daughter, beyond the most profound shock and sadness anyone can feel, seeing her death as mystery was all I was able to initially conclude. A difference between my father's death and the death of my daughter, however, was my father's was expected and "due" in the sense of age and having lived a full life. My daughter's death was unexpected and terribly premature. My family's world was placed very quickly out of balance. How could this event ever be atoned?

Slowly returning to the conversations with Sidney Keith and Martin High Bear many years before, I began to try to find a framework in which to find meaning in Felicity's death. Something about the Lakota understanding of *Wakan* at the time of death began to take shape.

The death of an individual in a traditional Lakota community or *tiospaye,* was an extremely significant event. Death was, certainly, well understood in the physical sense. It was a part of all life and, therefore, *Wakan,* but the loss was also understood as an occurrence that disrupted the balance of life which was important to understanding *Wakan.* The loss of anyone in the *tiospaye* was impactful because each member represented an accumulation of unique, important, insight into community survival and experience.

\*\*\*\*\*\*

*When asking one's age in Lakota, one says "Waniyetu nitonakca hwo" (How many winters are you?). Winter represented the most dangerous of seasons for the Lakota. An individual's knowledge and wisdom accumulated over many years was acknowledged and respected. Thus, when asking or answering, the number of winters survived was an indicator of the knowledge, skill, and wisdom possessed. The importance of this was that the qualities that brought a person to older age were also the qualities that would allow all of the tiospaye to survive. When the individual died, the tiospaye recognized the loss to the family and community on many levels.* – conversation with Calvin Jumping Bull

\*\*\*\*\*\*

The interrelatedness and dependency of the entire *tiospaye* on each individual member was profoundly recognized by the Lakota. The loss of a member of the family and community threatened the ability of all, in a sense, to survive. The deceased's significance, then, was understood in very meaningful ways. The loss of balance, in both a philosophical and well as practical sense, had to be compensated for in terms of the roles of the survivors and prayer for assistance from the *Wakan* to bring physical and spiritual balance back to the family and community of the deceased.

The death of a Lakota was accompanied, as in most American Indian and other societies worldwide, by practices regarding the physical remains of the deceased as well the spiritual legacy. The deceased was dressed in their best clothing, purified with the smoke of sweet-grass or sage, and the body was wrapped in buffalo or other available hides. Items of importance to the person in life were usually included with the body in the hide. The wrapped body was brought to a location remote from the *tiospaye* and placed in a tree or on a scaffold constructed for the purpose to protect it from animals. Before wrapping the body, however, a lock of hair was removed and placed inside a small bundle or wrap of hide.

Native American Historical Collection, Library of Congress

The *sicun* (the spirit of the deceased) is the focus of Lakota belief and ceremony following the removal and burial placement of the body of the deceased. The immediate spiritual impact of a death, as well as the ceremonies, are about the eventual journey of the deceased's spirit along the spirit road (*wanagi canku;* also the Milky Way). This spirit is contained by the lock of hair removed after death.  Following the removal of the deceased's *sicun,* the body may be taken away to return to the earth.

*Sicun* is the spirit housed within a Lakota and given at birth. The *sicun* may be the spirit of anything and may be chosen by a *pejuta wicasa*, appear in someone's dream, or through association with an occurrence around the time of birth. One's *sicun* may provide an early name for the child. The *sicun* is immortal and is present to help and protect the individual throughout their life. Additional *sicun* may be acquired in life and may be accompanied by new names, but it is believed to be only the original *sicun* that travels to the world of spirits after death.

\*\*\*\*\*\*

*A Sicun is like a spirit. It is the ton-ton sni, that is, it is immortal and cannot die. A Lakota may have many Sicunpi, but he always has one. It is Wakan, that is, it is like Wakan Tanka. It may be the spirit of anything.*
– One Star in *Internet Sacred Texts Archive*

\*\*\*\*\*\*

The bundle with the deceased's lock of hair is kept by their family as the spirit (*sicun*) of the loved one for a period of time. The period of time may differ from situation to situation, but it was most commonly kept for approximately one year. The presence of the *sicun* was of comfort to the loved ones and allowed both to become comfortable with the mystery (*Wakan*) soon to follow.

\*\*\*\*\*\*

*It is good to have a reminder of death before us, for it helps us to understand the impermanence of life on this earth, and this understanding may aid us in preparing for our own death. He who is well prepared is he who knows that he is nothing compared with Wakan Tanka, who is everything; then he knows that world which is real."* — Black Elk in *The Sacred Pipe*

******

It may be recalled that the first of the sacred rites of the pipe brought to the Lakota was the *Wanagi Kiciyuha* ( Keeping of the Spirit).  This refers to the initial rite and period of time when the family of the deceased kept the bundle with the lock of hair (*sicun*/spirit) as well as the "releasing" of the spirit at the end of this period; sometimes called the *Istamni Pakinte* (Wiping of Tears) ceremony.

The keeping of the spirit was a fundamental component of the grieving process. The "keeper of the spirit", usually the parent, the spouse, or child of the deceased, had very clear responsibilities regarding the spirit in the form of the bundle containing the lock of hair. The bundle was not seen as a memento or personal object of the loved one. Indeed, the bundle contained the actual spirit which was kept by the family for the first portion of the grief process. In a sense, the loved one had physically died, but the spirit remained alive and with the family. The spirit bundle, then, needed to be protected, honored, and handled appropriately. This period of a spirit's life following physical death was of tremendous comfort to the loved ones of the deceased.

\*\*\*\*\*\*

*With our spiritual beliefs we know we have him (her brother), not physically, but spiritually. He is still with us. We believe in that. In grieving that really helps us – knowing that all things are living in one way or another.*
*– Suzie Eagle Staff* in *Lakota Grieving*

\*\*\*\*\*\*

The period of time was marked by great sadness and sorrow shared by the entire *tiospaye* with the family. It was expected that the grief would be expressed openly, frequently, and publicly.

No one was to be embarrassed by such demonstrations of sorrow. Community expectations about the grief process made expressions of grief understandable and appropriate.

After a time, again, usually about a year after the death, when the keeper felt that this initial period of grief was to end, the spirit was released to continue its journey to *wanagiyata*. The rite of the pipe surrounding the release of the spirit is complex and involved the presence of the entire *tiospaye* which shared the grief of the keeper. The ceremony involved prayers to the spirit to remember the living communicated through the sacred pipe.

*****

*The keeper of the pipe then walks around to the south and, picking up the "soul bundle," says to it: "Grandchild, you are about to leave on a great journey. Your father and mother and all your relatives have loved you. Soon they will be happy."* – Black Elk in *The Sacred Pipe*

******

At the conclusion of the ceremony, the spirit bundle is taken outside of the lodge and opened. At this moment, the spirit is "released" and is no longer inside the bundle. The bundle and lock of hair may be kept by the keeper as a remembrance or may be burned. The spirit travels along the pathway in the sky we recognize as the Milky Way to the land of the spirits which is a part of all things and is *Wakan*.

The release of the spirit from its special time with loved ones marks a formalized progression of grief into a joy and happiness, for the deceased is now a greater part of all that is Wakan, Wakan Tanka, the great mystery; that which cannot be understood by humankind. The Lakota spend little time dwelling on any details of the spirit world (*wanagiyata*) or attempts to describe it. We cannot understand and it is that which makes it *Wakan*. The journey of the spirit is now complete and has returned the balance in the world after the loss of the loved one. That balance is also *Wakan*.

# Part Ten: Understanding Grief: The Context of Our Religious Traditions

I don't pretend to understand death and grief. I'm pretty sure I don't understand it as a concept. I'm really sure I don't understand my own grief or that of my wife or that of Felicity's older brothers. I am also certain that I don't understand how they are going about the task of gaining an equilibrium that seems to be eluding me. Perhaps they are not and I am just so mired that I can't see where they are in this. I have a circle of acquaintances that have wisely advised us that, in particular, spouses grieve differently, at differing paces, and with differing levels of visibility. I am hopeful that this is the case as it is immensely comforting.

\*\*\*\*\*\*

*Be kind, for everyone you meet is carrying a great burden.* – Attributed to Philo in *Kayak Morning*

\*\*\*\*\*\*

I have come to understand, however, that there is a difference between grief protocols and actual grieving. There are those things we do and those things we feel.  In most cases, there is probably congruence between them. I suspect that this was easier to observe in times past and in smaller communities. It is clear, however, that the greater the clarity of belief, the less likely is the dissonance between the protocols and their foundation in belief and grieving.

Many, however, despite a reasonable strength of faith, find that grief and loss are very difficult feelings to manage, particularly after our communities have moved on and we feel we are on our own at some point. We find that the grief protocols prescribed by our religious traditions only take us so far, both in terms of comfort, but also in answering important questions that we cannot avoid. We struggle with the questions that swirl around in our grief that our religious traditions are supposed to answer. Does a heaven or other form of afterlife exist? What is it like? Is a hell a real possibility? How does one know? Should I pray for the loved one or should I pray to them? Are remedies and protocols of my religion for the benefit of my loved one or are they for me? Does my community really care beyond the initial support it provided? Does my community understand how deep the sadness and sorrow I feel? Do others feel my loss too? Does my community mourn? Does it cry like me? All are questions the grieving ask daily. The answers do not seem to appear, but we are asked to have faith. We don't know that answers will arrive, but maybe they will someday. On the other hand, have we been asking the wrong questions or are there no answers?

I have, over the years and, as explained in previous sections, come to be familiar with Lakota protocols surrounding death and grief.  If my understanding of the teachings of Sidney Keith and Martin High Bear concerning *Wakan* is indeed their understanding and belief, I think I have come to understand death and grief philosophically in Lakota as well and I believe that this has informed my continuing struggle with understanding the loss of my daughter.

While this is rather presumptuous, Sidney and Martin would likely forgive me. Lakotas understand the individuality that is a foundation of spirituality. The idea of *Wakan* as mystery, and even the unknowable, permits the necessary individuality and ambiguity of grief even in the context of the involvement of one's *tiospaye*.  Further, acceptance of not knowing encourages one to be open to new feelings and possibilities rather than, perhaps, limited by the certainty that western religion attempts to show.

In my case, the openness results in greater insight. Although I never expect to recover from my sadness and loss over the death of my daughter, the idea of *Wakan* has helped my healing.

# Part 11: Understanding Grief and Grieving in the Context of Lakota Wakan

A fundamental premise of Lakota belief is that *Wakan* is anything we cannot understand in our world and in our lives and we were never meant to understand. Because of this, death, even though we believe we understand it physically, cannot be understood spiritually. This premise leads to several assertions about *Wakan* and the role the understanding of *Wakan* can play in assisting the grief process.

I. Lakota belief will not attempt to answer the questions asked in Part 10. The comfort in what is *Wakan* is that no attempt is made to answer questions that really cannot be answered as much as we would like, and feel we need to know. *Wakan* implies the acceptance of not knowing and taking comfort in that lack of knowledge. *Wakan* provides no protocols of belief; no set of standard beliefs created by others. It assumes that all things related to the spirituality of death are a great mystery. They are sacred because of their association with that great mystery. In the Western tradition, this perspective seems so counter-intuitive. Wouldn't greater knowledge be more likely to bring greater closure over the death? I believe Lakota understanding would conclude that it does not. The information and resulting insight is simply not accessible.

******

*Death is a great teacher. Don't be afraid of death. Let it free you.* – Michael A. Singer in *The Untethered Soul*

******

II. I would suggest that Christianity, to one degree or another based on denomination, appropriately recognizes the mystery that exists in human death and its role in grief. It is assumed, however, that a godly rationale exists; a reason determined by a loving god. That

Christian belief incorporates the idea of the mystery in much of what is to be believed is important and suggests a belief in a greater power that is much more complex and uncertain than the trappings of Christianity seem to project. The notion of mystery in Christianity also suggests the complexity that exists in the development of Christianity and the impact or influence of other major world religions. The inclusivity of this history, intentional or not, is not to be overlooked. Wakan takes the above to another destination, however, where the mystery of a greater power may not exist. Wakan is simply a mystery and it is the not knowing that provides the sacred in Lakota belief.

******

*God moves in mysterious ways.*
— William Cowper

******

**III.** Very importantly, the acknowledgement of *Wakan* largely eliminates feelings of self-blame as well as a search to find blame somewhere in explaining the death of a loved one. Guilt suggests the existence of a cause and effect. In my case, what role did I have in my daughter's death? What could I have done to prevent this loss? Why didn't I do it? As a father, why couldn't I protect and care for my daughter so that the accident wouldn't have occurred? Was I a real father to my daughter? All of these thoughts have certainly passed through my head, but the mystery of it all in *Wakan* has led me to be more comfortable in not knowing. It is the way of *Wakan*.

******

Man knows much more than he understands.
– Alfred Adler in *Alfred Adler Revisited*

******

Additionally, the idea of *Wakan* eases the very negative tendency to blame someone, something, or many others and other things for what occurred. Everyone from the driver of the semi-truck, to inadequate roads in southern Minnesota, to the whole area where she lived, and even to Felicity herself for not paying attention to her driving, not taking precautions, seemingly not caring......... Blame has no place when all is *Wakan* and unknowable.

Certainly, in traditional Lakota communities, consequences for perpetrators existed when harm to another or the community was intentional, including banishment from the *tiospaye*. Blame, however, was viewed as counter-productive and unjustifiable in most all other circumstances.

**IV.** Lakota understanding of the grief process as represented by the Keeping of the Spirit rite of the sacred pipe bears some similarity to other religious traditions where there is an extended period of time for certain aspects of the grieving process. Among Lakota, the importance of believing that the spirit of the deceased remains with the family members and *tiospaye* for an extended period of time recognizes and institutionalizes the understanding that grieving takes a great deal of time. It is understood that there is no benefit or reason to hurry grieving with the goal of "getting over it" as soon as possible. It also reminds the community of the continuing needs of the loved ones of the deceased and the appropriateness of public expressions of grief that these individuals may express. The emotions attending to grief do not have to occur only in private. The community expects the family members to experience the waves of grief that are a part of everyone's grief experience. No one believes that public grieving is anything but the natural way of grief. Grief is honored and respected in Lakota communities.

****** 

*Time alone does not automatically see people through all the grieving tasks. Grieving takes work. But the work takes time.* – Stephen Huffstetter, SCJ in *Lakota Grieving*

\*\*\*\*\*\*

**V.** The "Wiping of Tears" ceremony, described earlier and the conclusion of the ongoing rite of the "Keeping of the Spirit", celebrates the practical return to the grieving individuals to the everyday life of their welcoming community. As the *sicun* of the deceased is released to follow the *wanagi canku*, knowing that the time was coming, the family and other grievers are prepared for the transition from personal grief to accepting grief and loss in the context of their community. This event can also be seen as a symbolic return to the balance of *Wakan* that was disrupted by the loss of the deceased to the family and the community.

**VI.** The Lakota emphasis on grieving that is as relevant to the whole community (*tiospaye*) as it is to those individuals closest to the deceased can be seen as particularly comforting. Recognizing the role of one's *tiospaye* in the understanding of loss and grieving was clear to the Lakota. The Wiping of Tears celebrating the release of the deceased's *sicun* was usually accompanied by a giveaway (*wihpeyapi*). A Lakota giveaway is associated with many life events where the family of the person being honored gives away household items, money, and culturally important items such as blankets, beadwork and quillwork, and even horses at a gathering of the community.  When associated with the end of the Keeping of the Spirit period, the possessions of the deceased may be given away in honor of the loved one. This expression notes the loss of the individual to the family and community to the detriment of the balance within *Wakan* and the restoration of the balance through the distribution of the deceased's possessions. The giveaway is also an opportunity to provide assistance to the individuals and families of the community that are in the greatest need through a redistribution of the wealth of the deceased.

**VII.**  Everything is really one thing and that is the great mystery, *Wakan Tanka.* This concept has, perhaps, had the greatest relevance to me. As noted previously, I desperately want to know that our daughter is still with us. If everything is one thing, it is clear that nothing is ever lost from the hoop of the world in Black Elk's vision, not even death.

Lakotas often begin and end a speech, greeting, or a prayer with the invocation of *Mitakuye Oyasin* (All my relatives) which reminds all that, as a Lakota, I am related to all present, all peoples, all spirits, and all existing in the world. Life and death are one thing as is everything *Wakan*. The state of death is another state of life as is the reverse. Both are the same in different forms. The deceased and the living have a shared concern for loved ones, *tiospaye*, and all one's relations.

******

*I am going to present our rituals to give an understanding of their basic purpose, the essence of which can be expressed most clearly in the phrase Mitakuye Oyasin. This translates as "all my relatives" or*

*"we are all related." It is an often-used phrase in our culture. Our philosophy and way of life are based on it, and I hope you will give it some thought.*
– Albert White Hat in *Life's Journey - Zuya*

******

**IX.**  The Lakota translation of "heaven" is loosely *wanagiyata,* , the land of the spirits. It is clear, however, that Lakota belief does not assume this to be an actual place (spiritually speaking) or a world that is separate from that of the living. There is no feeling that special things are enjoyed or suffered in this other world by those that have passed on. *Wanagiyata,* perhaps, may be best thought of as a kind of life rather than a place.

**X.**  Lakota belief in the "inseparability" of all things implied in the vision of the hoop of the world and the interrelatedness of all things as in the concept of *mitakuye oyasin,* means that the *sicun* of the deceased is among us at all times. When the *sicun* is released from its special attachment to the individual's family by way of the Keeping of the Soul rite and the Wiping of Tears, the *sicun* is being released into the larger world shared by the living. Thus, the *sicun*, the spirit of the deceased, is always among us, not just the period of time with the family. The deceased, then, continue to guide us, assist us, support us, receive our prayers, act on our prayers, and comfort us in the knowing that they are indeed always among us. We are reminded of this through signs of their presence and through the visibility brought about by the intervention and communication of the medicine men such as Sidney Keith and Martin High Bear.

# Part Eleven: Some Final Thoughts

I hope it is clear by this time that I am not discussing the notion of *Wakan* and Lakota spirituality as an alternative to other ways of addressing grief whether through established religion or secular means. I am suggesting, however, that, at least for me, the available religious and secular means are not satisfying. They have been helpful, but did not go far enough in assisting my grief over Felicity.

As I have mentioned previously, my Catholic tradition (or more accurately, that of my wife's) was aimed at providing answers. I felt, however, the answers were such that I could not know how they could be arrived at other than through an assertion of faith that I could not provide. This is not to say the Catholic liturgy and protocols of our families are incorrect or ill-intended, just not personally adequate.

No one should, however, distrust their beliefs about death and afterlife based on what has been shared in this narrative. All recognized and unrecognized religions, beliefs, and other spiritual communities respond to the phenomenon of death. Additionally, a substantial literature and practice in understanding grief exists based in the humanities and professional disciplines. One should seek understanding from wherever and whoever offers assistance and comfort.

I have found that such assistance often originates from unanticipated places. This includes the individual understanding among those who work with the families of the deceased and are experienced in comforting them even though it is not in the job description. Such encounters, in retrospect, have fit very well into the world view of the Lakota and the idea of *Wakan*. As an example,

Morrie Toretsky manages a small cemetery monument shop that we found ,or more accurately, found us. When we walked in the shop, the first thing we saw was a monument previously engraved that was being used as a showroom model. Please note from the photo of it below that it was etched with the family name of Mathieu and the husband's name of Raymond which, coincidentally perhaps, was also my father's name.

The shock of the seeming coincidence was broken by Morrie's soft voice telling us, "It appears you are in the right place." When not talking about the details of selecting a monument and assisting with our choice, he spoke of his garden and his tomatoes of which he was very proud as well as his wife who wanted him to retire soon. Morrie was a very important part of sharing our grief and knew what he could provide. The memory is as comforting now as it was the day we walked into Morrie's shop.

What I have shared about the Lakota and my journey thus far is a vision learned long ago, but only recently understood. Sidney Keith, Martin High Bear, and most of the other Lakota traditionalists who enriched my understanding of death and grief are now deceased themselves. I would like to think that it was their *sicun* that is now a part of everything, brought me back to their time with me to assist me with thinking about unimaginable loss and the grieving that I continue to experience.

I remain open to new insights into the event of Felicity's death. I believe and welcome any signs from my daughter, my thoughts, or the "universe" that she is OK; that she does not suffer because of the suffering I and other are experiencing resulting from the loss of this beautiful girl and beautiful spirit. I look for these signs every day, not knowing if they will occur or what they might mean.

My wife and I attended several sessions of a grief support group a few months after the death of our daughter. The experience was a good one in many ways. The other participants had all lost children who had been adults or young adults at the time of their death.  We were struck by a commonality that all of the participants appeared to have experienced. There was, in each case, some small aspect seemingly inconsequential or coincidental outside of the context of the individual, unique to the deceased that reappeared after their death. One set of parents mentioned they find purple "Skittles" candy occasional in their house where they had not appeared earlier. These purple candies were the favorite of their late daughter. Others, including my wife and me, have experienced such "signs" of the presence of our loved one. An occasional whiff of her favorite perfume, and occasional glances from Daisy and Dixie, her cats who now live with us, that go beyond them and seem so similar to Felicity's communicating via her glance or her stare.

*Wakanheja,* which means children in Lakota, suggests the special relationship of babies, children, and young adults to their parents. Children, themselves, are *Wakan* and represent the future of the family and the *tiospaye*. The loss of a child was seen by the Lakota as the most significant of deaths. The loss to the community was of great importance as well as the loss of what might have been .

The word *wakanheja* is a most meaningful term in Lakota in the context of grief over the loss of a child. There is mystery with the birth and development of a child. There is mystery in how a child becomes a part of a community, yet also as an individual. There is mystery in all that a child encounters that contributes to who they become. There is mystery in the special skills and understandings that the child will bring to the lives of the community and the well-being of all. A child is the hope of a family and a community. It is also the verification that *Lakota* includes all who ever were and all that ever will be. The loss of a child is not just the loss of someone as they were, but also losing what the child meant in terms of a future they will never have among the living. Death (*t'e*) changes expectations and anticipations from the real to the not real (*kte*). This is especially difficult, but the *Wakan* that binds everything makes the reality of death into, perhaps, new expectations and realities of the role of the deceased in our lives and all that is *Wakan*.

I have used my shared understanding of *Wakan* as a door to deeper understanding of death and its impact on others close to the deceased and their community. This was also, I hope not selfishly, for me. I now believe deeply that Felicity's death was sacred because it was *Wakan* and the attribution of sacredness to anything associated with *Wakan* is *ton*. Felicity's *sicun* is still close to us, but will one day be released to become a part of all creation. I am proud to say and believe *Mitakuye Oyasin*.

*Pilamaya yelo.*

# About
# Felicity Abby Jane Mathieu
# (Lissy)

Felicity was born in 1984 in Mitchell, South
Dakota. With our family, she moved to Akita,
Japan where she attended Kindergarten
through 4th grade at Kawazoe Shogako
(elementary school) and became fluent in
Japanese. After graduation from Prior Lake High
School (Minnesota), Felicity graduated from
Normandale Community College and served as
a special education paraprofessional educator
for several years. While working a full-time job,
Felicity went on to receive her bachelor's
degree (posthumously) from Walden University
with majors in Non-profit Management and
Women's Studies.

Sue Ann's stories of Lissy tell of her caring little
for prestige, pointless drama, and the "good
life" of wealth as represented by the

"Housewives of Atlanta, Los Angeles, New Jersey, Des Moines, etc. - shows which she sometimes watched as comedies. As Sue Ann said at the funeral, Lissy preferred rural life, regular folk with regular lives, children that face challenges, and critters that needed homes.

Lissy died nearly instantly at 10:30 am on February 1st, 2012 when her car and a semi-tractor-trailer collided head-on on a foggy and icy, two-lane highway in rural southern Minnesota. Her ashes are divided between a suburban cemetery in the Twin Cities and the Kurose Zen Buddhist Hondo (temple) in Yuwa-town, Akita-prefecture, Japan.

Her name continues with Ben's daughter and our granddaughter, Yuna Felicity Mathieu.

# Lakota Pronunciation Information

The orthography (writing system) of the Lakota words used in this narrative was created by the author for use in classroom teaching materials where an easy-to-type system was needed.  It is based on the lexigraphical Dakota orthographies used by Stephen Return Riggs from the 1850s and the Lakota version used by the Jesuit, Fr. Eugene Buechel in the 1880s. The orthography used here is also similar to that used by the Dakota Language Program at the University of Minnesota.

The following pronunciations of Lakota consonants and vowels are somewhat simplified below to allow the reader some notion as to pronunciation without the benefit of hearing the language orally. The pronunciations are compared to examples from English.

There are five vowel sounds in Lakota and are represented with

a    as in *father*

e    as in *they* or as a long *a* as in *date*

i    as in *marine* or as a long *e* as in *we*

o    as in *go*

u    as in *rude* or as a double *o* as in *mood*

An exception occurs when the vowel is immediately followed by an *n.* In such cases, the vowel is "nasalized" as in many French vowel sounds such as *sans, bon, bien,* and *un.*

The majority of consonant sounds in Lakota are similar to those in English and use their English equivalents with a couple of exceptions.

c    is always pronounced *ch* as in *china.*

j    is always pronounced as a soft *j* as in the *g* in *age*

s    may be pronounced as an English *s* in

some words and as an *sh* in others.

There are, however, several consonant sounds in Lakota that do not have English equivalents. The consonants *h* and *g* may be pronounced as they are in English in some words, but may be pronounced as "velars" in others. In the latter, air is moved between the back of the tongue and the *velum* or back of the roof of the mouth. This creates, when pronouncing a velar *g* or velar *h*, a vibration similar to that in a German *ch* sound as in *bauch*.

Additionally, there are several Lakota consonants that may, in some words, use a full "glottal stop" where the glottis is quickly closed to very briefly interrupt the sound and reopened to complete the word. Glottal stops may occur with the letters *t, s, k, p,* velar *g,* and velar *h.* I have marked these with an apostrophe as in *t'e* (dead). One last pronunciation guide – emphasis is always placed on either the first or second syllable of any Lakota word.

# Bibliographic References

Bad Hand, Howard P. (2002). *Native American Healing: A Lakota Ritual*, Dog Soldier Press, Taos, New Mexico.

Brokenleg, Martin and David Middleton, "Native Americans: Adapting, Yet Retaining," in Irish, Donald P., Lundquist, Kathleen F., and Nelson, Vivian Jenkins (eds.) (1993). *Ethnic Variations in Dying, Death, and Grief*, Taylor and Francis, Washington, DC.

Brown, Joseph Epes (1953). *The Sacred Pipe: Black Elk's Account of the Seven Rites of the Oglala Sioux*, University of Oklahoma Press, Norman.

Buechel, Eugene, S.J. (1970*). A Dictionary of The Teton Dakota Sioux Language*, Red Cloud Indian School, Pine Ridge, SD.

Carlson, Jon and Michael P. Maniacci, Eds. (2012). *Alfred Adler Revisited*, Routledge, New York.

Deloria, Vine, Jr. (2006). *The World We Used to Live in: Remembering the Powers of the Medicine Men*, Fulcrum Publishing, Golden, CO.

Hare, John. "NATIVE AMERICAN RELIGIONS". Internet Sacred Texts Archive. http://www.sacred-texts.com/nam/index.htm. Retrieved 12 November 2012.

Huffstetter, Stephen, SCJ (1998). *Lakota Grieving*, Tipi Press, St. Joseph's Indian School, Chamberlain, SD.

Keith, Sidney (1975). *Sioux Dictionary*, Sioux Nation Arts Council, Eagle Butte, SD.

Mathieu, David J., Bertha Chasing Hawk, and Elgin Badwound (1977). *Lakota Language I*, Black Hills State College, Spearfish, S.D.

Mathieu, David J., Bertha Chasing Hawk, and Elgin Badwound (1977). *Lakota Language II,* Black Hills State College, Spearfish, S.D.

Mathieu, David J. and Ray Howe (1976). "American Indian Studies as an Academic Discipline" in *Selected Papers of the Midwestern Ethnic Studies Conference.* University of Wisconsin Press, La Crosse.

Momaday, N. Scott (1969). *The Way to Rainy Mountain,* University of New Mexico Press, Santa Fe.

Niehardt, John G. (1932). *Black Elk Speaks: Being the Life Story of a Holy Man of the Oglala Sioux,* University of Nebraska Press, Lincoln.

Rosenblatt, Roger (2012). *Kayak Morning,* HarperCollins, New York.

Singer, Michael A. (2007). *The Untethered Soul: The Journey Beyond Yourself,* Noetic Books, Oakland, CA.

Theisz, R.D. (1975). *Buckskin Tokens: Contemporary Oral Narratives of the Lakota,* Sinte Gleska College, Rosebud, SD.

Thomas, Kevin (2012). *A Common Man (Ikce Wicasa): Modern Lakota Spirituality and Practice Words and Wisdom from Sidney Keith and Melvin Miner*, Book Baby, Kindle Edition.

Walker, James R. (1980). *Lakota Belief and Ritual.* Edited by R.J. DeMallie and E. Jahner, University of Nebraska Press, Lincoln.

White Hat, Albert, Sr. (2012). *Life's Journey – Zuya: Oral Teachings from the Rosebud,* University of Utah Press, Salt Lake City.

Young Bear, Severt and R.D. Theisz. (1993). *Standing in the Light: A Lakota Way of Seeing,* University of Nebraska Press, Lincoln.

## About the Author

David Mathieu has been a professor and senior administrator at the university level for nearly 40 years in private and public higher education institutions in several states and overseas in Japan.

Dr. Mathieu's teaching background has focused on American Indian Studies and, more specifically, Lakota Language, American Indian tribal government, tribal law and American Indian policy, American Indian education methods, history and culture. *Way of Wakan* is his fifth book. The others include two Lakota language textbooks (*Lakota Language I & II*), *Introduction to Indian Education,* and *Emerging Together: Biculturalism and American Indian Education.* He has additionally written numerous articles on tribal subjects as well as many presentations.

Since moving into senior academic and student affairs administration, almost 25 years ago, Dr. Mathieu's writings and presentations have focused on several areas of higher education policy and university administration such as enrollment management, higher education branding and marketing, general education and ethnic studies curricula, faculty development, institutional governance, and institutional finance.  He retired from university administration in the summer of 2012.

David and Sue Ann Daley-Mathieu have been married for 40 years and, in addition to their late daughter, have two grown children, three grandchildren, and two step-grandchildren. In the 90s, David and the family lived in Japan for about 4 ½ years. It is probably not surprising that two of his children have Japanese spouses and all maintain strong ties to Japan.

# Notes

Notes

# Notes

# Notes

Notes

Notes

Notes